Write On...
VOLCANOES

Clare Hibbert

W

FRANKLIN WATTS
LONDON·SYDNEY

Franklin Watts
First published in Great Britain in 2016 by The Watts Publishing Group

Credits
Series Editor: Melanie Palmer
Conceived and produced by Hollow Pond
Editor: Clare Hibbert @ Hollow Pond
Designer: Amy McSimpson @ Hollow Pond
Illustrations: Kate Sheppard
Photographs: Alamy: 4-5 (JTB Media Creation, Inc), 6-7 (Michele Falzone),
11 (ROPI), 13 (Benny Marty), 15 (World History Archive), 19 (Arctic Images),
20-21 (Tom Uhlman), 23 (Ace Stock Ltd), 25 (robertharding), 26-27 (National
Geographic Creative); Shutterstock: cover (Catmando), 8t (Santi Rodriguez),
17 (mtree555), 29 (Allies Interactive), 29tr (khd), 29b (JeniFoto).
Every attempt has been made to clear copyright. Should there be any
inadvertent omission please apply to the publisher for rectification.

ISBN 978 1 4451 5012 3

Printed in China

FSC
www.fsc.org
MIX
Paper from
responsible sources
FSC® C104740

Franklin Watts
An imprint of
Hachette Children's Group
Part of The Watts Publishing Group
Carmelite House
50 Victoria Embankment
London EC4Y 0DZ

An Hachette UK Company
www.hachette.co.uk

www.franklinwatts.co.uk

Look out for the **Write On...** writing tips and tools scattered
through the book, then head to the Writing school on page 28
for project ideas to inspire your awesome inner author.

Write On...
VOLCANOES

CONTENTS

What is a volcano?

A volcano is a place where hot, liquid rock bursts out of the ground. This is called an eruption. At this very moment, at least twenty volcanoes are erupting around the world.

A volcano that is erupting now or has erupted recently is called an active volcano. There are around 1,500 active volcanoes. During an eruption, the volcano may throw out glowing, molten rock called lava, as well as ash, rocks and mud. The lava is a scorching 1,000 °C – ten times hotter than boiling water.

Making mountains

Volcanoes usually look like mountains or hills. The lava and ash that erupted in the past slowly build up to make a mountain shape with sloping sides.

The world's most active volcano is Kilauea on the island of Hawaii. It's quite young for a volcano – between 300,000 and 600,000 years old!

Mount Asama in Japan had two huge eruptions in 1108 and 1783. It is still active today.

Volcanoes are named after Vulcan, the god of fire in Roman mythology. He had a forge under a volcano.

Write On...

Take out a book of myths from the library. Find the story of Vulcan or another god or hero. Retell it, but set it in the present day.

Volcano hot spots

Volcanoes have been erupting ever since the Earth was newly formed, billions of years ago. They have shaped our planet. Most volcanoes are found at places where two sections of Earth's crust meet.

Earth's crust is its outer surface. It is made up of sections called plates, which float on a layer of hot, molten rock called magma. In places where two plates are moving away from each other, magma rises out of the gap. It forms volcanoes. Magma can also surface at a boundary where one plate is pushing under another plate.

The Pacific Ring of Fire

Three-quarters of the world's active volcanoes are along the plate boundaries on the edges of the Pacific Ocean. No wonder the area is called the Pacific Ring of Fire!

There are volcanoes on other planets, too. The largest one in the Solar System is Olympus Mons on Mars.

Volcanoes that form in the middle of plates are called hot spots. Magma (see page 10) has to push harder here, as there's no gap to fill.

Don't just use rhyming words in poems. Pepper any writing with them, to give it more of a rhythm. Try **crust** and **dust**, **plate** and **late** or **hot** and **shot**.

Indonesia, which has about 130 volcanoes, is part of the Pacific Ring of Fire. These ones are on the island of Java.

Mount Semeru

Shapes and features

Volcanoes come in different shapes and sizes. The most common shape is the cinder cone – a cone-shaped mountain with a wide crater at the top. Low, wide volcanoes are called shield volcanoes.

A shield volcano on Tenerife, in the Canary Islands

 The hot, liquid lava comes out of a central tube, called a vent.

 The vent is connected by a pipe to an underground chamber of magma.

 The flanks (slopes) of the volcano are made up of layers of old, cooled lava.

 Some volcanoes have side vents, called dykes.

 A violent eruption can blow away a huge chunk of the volcano, leaving a big hollow called a caldera.

 A caldera that fills with water is called a crater lake.

Write On...

Think of a mountain shape when you plan a story. On the upward slope, set the scene and start the action. At the peak, make your characters face a problem. On the downward slope, solve the problem and tie up any loose ends.

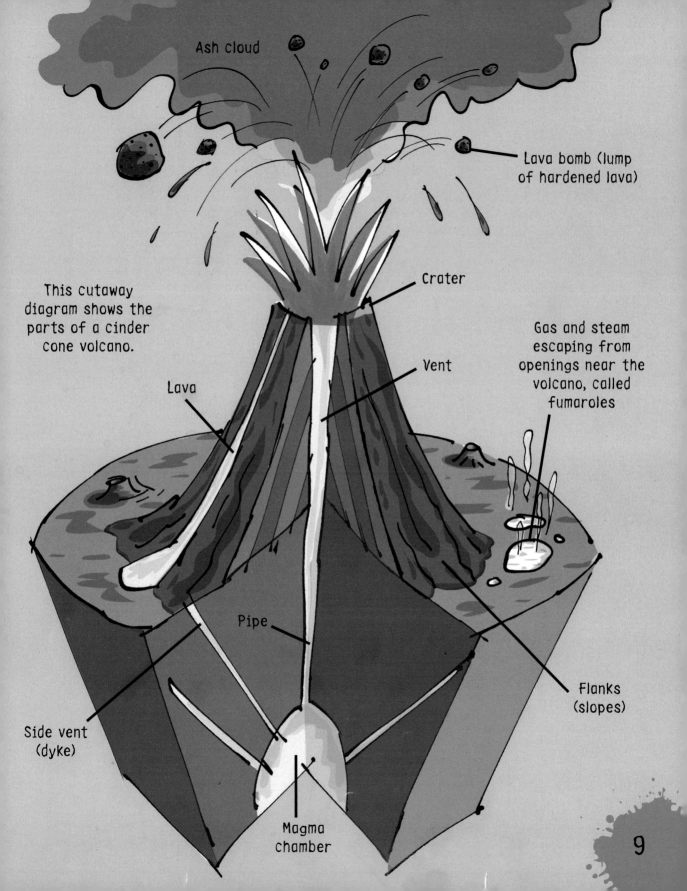

Ash cloud

Lava bomb (lump of hardened lava)

This cutaway diagram shows the parts of a cinder cone volcano.

Crater

Gas and steam escaping from openings near the volcano, called fumaroles

Lava

Vent

Pipe

Flanks (slopes)

Side vent (dyke)

Magma chamber

9

Eruption!

An eruption happens after magma – molten rock inside the Earth – has built up under a volcano. The magma is usually released in a sudden, violent explosion, and can be more powerful than a nuclear bomb.

As magma bubbles and swells under the volcano, so does the pressure. Some lava might even leak out of the sides of the volcano. Eventually, the pressure of the magma is too great. The volcano erupts!

Boom!

Pressurised magma and gas shoot out of the volcano. At the same time, ash, dust and chunks of rock are thrown into the sky. The eruption releases an enormous amount of heat and energy. Eruptions can last days or even years.

Volcanoes unlikely to erupt again are called extinct. Volcanoes that aren't active but might erupt in the future are called dormant (sleeping).

When molten rock is inside the Earth, it is called magma. Once it erupts from a volcano, it is called lava.

Mount Etna is a volcano on the Italian island of Sicily. This eruption was on 5 August 2014.

Write On...

Write a news report about a volcanic eruption. Before you start, brainstorm what facts readers will want to know, such as where and when it happened, and when the volcano had last erupted.

All sorts of lava

Lava is the hot, liquid rock that erupts out of a volcano. It can shoot into the sky as a dramatic fire fountain, rush down the sides of the volcano or flow out more slowly.

Lava can be thick and sticky or thin and runny. It forms a river that flows away from the volcano. The lava can travel many kilometres before it cools and stops. Sometimes a hardened 'skin' forms on top of the lava, but the lava keeps moving underneath.

Cool rocks

When the lava cools, it hardens into different kinds of rock. Thick, slow-moving lava forms jagged blocks called aa (say *ah*). Runny, fast-flowing lava forms smooth-surfaced pahoehoe (say *pa-hoey-hoey*).

Thin, runny lava can speed down the side of a volcano at up to 100 km/h.

Pele (say *Pay–lay*) is a fire goddess in Hawaiian mythology. Small lava bombs – flying lava lumps – are nicknamed Pele's tears.

Write On...

Alliteration (repeating the same sound at the start of a word) makes your writing more interesting. Examples are **fire fountain**, **fast-flowing** and **lava lumps**. You try some.

Fiery lava flows into the sea from Kilauea, an active shield volcano on Hawaii.

Clouds of ash

In 2010 a volcanic eruption in Iceland created a huge, spreading cloud of ash. Most flights over Europe were cancelled for almost a week!

During a violent volcanic eruption, billowing grey ash can blast into the air. Sometimes the ash falls near the volcano, where it hardens into a rock called tuff; other times, the wind blows it far away.

Hot gases rushing out of the volcano fire the ash into the air. The ash is made up of tiny bits of rock. It can form a towering column up to 50 km high.

Ash avalanche

Sometimes the column collapses, sending an avalanche of hot ash, rock and gases rushing down the side of the volcano. This is called a pyroclastic flow. It zooms along at up to 700 km/h, destroying everything in its path.

Ash clouds sometimes contain bubbly lumps of lava that cool and harden into a light stone called pumice. People rub their feet with pumice to get rid of dead skin.

Write On...

An onomatopoeia (say *o-no-mat-o-pee-a*) is a word that sounds like its meaning. Try out **boom**, **bubble**, **rumble**, **whoosh** and **zoom**.

Ash erupts from Mount St Helens, USA, in 1980.

Funny features

The underground heat that causes volcanoes is called geothermal activity (*geo* means 'earth' and *thermal* means 'heat'). It creates many other features, too, including hot springs, steam holes, geysers and mud pools.

A geyser is where a fountain of boiling-hot water and steam suddenly spurts from the ground.

Fumaroles (see page 9) are openings in Earth's crust where gas and steam escapes. Some smell like rotten eggs.

Half of the world's active geysers are in Yellowstone Park in the United States. Eruptions from the tallest, Steamboat Geyser, reach 90 m.

Hot springs are called *onsen* in Japan. People bathe in them to relax.

Mud pools are hot springs that don't have much water, so the surface is just bubbling mud instead.

Write On...

Use a thesaurus to find some powerful alternative verbs to describe the action of a geyser. Try **spurt**, **gush**, **squirt**, **erupt**, **explode** and **shoot**.

Macaque monkeys in the cold north of Japan stay warm in hot springs.

Undersea eruptions

Volcanoes can be found under the sea. Like the ones on land, underwater volcanoes usually erupt along plate boundaries. Most undersea eruptions go unnoticed, but really large eruptions can create islands.

Many islands are the tops of extinct or active volcanoes – for example, the Hawaiian islands and Canary Islands. Hundreds of seamounts (underwater mountains) are also volcanoes. Lava from undersea eruptions cools fast and forms rounded clumps called pillow lava.

Black smokers

There are also volcanic hot springs on the ocean floor. Tall chimneys of black 'sand' build up around them, called black smokers. They provide a habitat for sulphur-eating bacteria. In turn, shrimps and giant tube worms feed on the bacteria.

Volcanic activity formed the island of Surtsey, off Iceland. It was named after the Norse god Surtr, king of the fire giants.

The Mid–Atlantic Ridge in the Atlantic Ocean is a plate boundary where two plates are pulling apart. Eruptions along this ridge push out magma and form new seabed.

Surtsey emerged from the sea in 1963. The eruption that created it went on for three-and-a-half years.

Write On...

Think about all five senses when you are setting the scene in a story. If you are diving to the seabed you won't be able to **taste** or **smell** anything, but what can you **see**, **hear** and **touch**?

Deadly dangers

Volcanoes can be destructive and dangerous. The flow of lava can kill people and animals and destroy buildings. Falling hot ash can suffocate people or spark fires.

Pyroclastic flows – speeding avalanches of hot ash, gas and rock – are even more deadly. They burn everything to a crisp. Volcanoes trigger other trouble, too. Mudflows happen when volcanic ash mixes with water. Volcanoes can also cause floods and tsunamis (tidal waves).

Measuring danger

The Volcanic Explosivity Index (VEI) measures how explosive a volcano is – and how dangerous. The highest level is a mega-colossal VEI 8 eruption. A VEI 8 only happens about once every 100,000 years.

Ash from Mount Merapi mixed with rainwater to form the mudflow that destroyed this Indonesian village.

In 1985, an entire Colombian town was buried by a mudflow caused by a volcanic eruption. Almost everyone died (around 22,000 people).

The 1815 eruption of Tambora in Indonesia was a VEI 7 eruption. It threw up so much ash that there was no sunshine the next summer.

Write On...

A haiku is a Japanese poem. It has three lines of five, seven and five syllables (beats). Here's one about a mudflow: see if you can try one too.

**Devastating, huge,
I swallow the helpless town
Mixing mud and snow.**

Poor Pompeii

Mount Vesuvius is an active volcano in Italy. Its most famous eruption happened in 79 CE. It was a catastrophe for the poor people who lived in the nearby town of Pompeii.

The 79 CE eruption was very explosive. It took the 11,000 people who lived in Pompeii completely by surprise. As they tried to run away, they were suffocated by falling ash.

Lost and found

Pompeii lay forgotten for centuries. From the 1750s, archaeologists started to dig it up. The Pomepiians' bodies had decayed, leaving people-shaped holes in the hardened ash. Archaeologists made models of the people — and even their pets! — by filling these holes with plaster.

A famous Roman writer called Pliny the Younger saw the eruption of Vesuvius from further up the coast. He wrote about it in his letters.

Vesuvius's last big eruption was about sixty years ago, but it is still active. More than half a million people live in the danger zone.

Write On...

Imagine witnessing a terrible natural disaster such as the eruption of Vesuvius. Like Pliny, describe what you see, but in an email not a letter. What words will help you show how shocking the event was?

Plaster models
of some of the
people who died in
Pompeii in 79 CE.

23

Useful volcanoes

Long ago, people may have settled on or near volcanoes without realising the dangers. But why do people *still* live near them today? The reason is that volcanic activity brings many useful gifts.

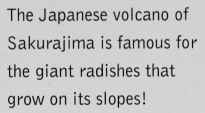

Farmers can grow bumper crops in volcanic soil. It contains ash and sulphur, which both help plants to grow.

The Japanese volcano of Sakurajima is famous for the giant radishes that grow on its slopes!

Geothermal energy from volcanic zones (see page 16) can be turned into electricity.

Sulphur mined from around volcanoes is used to make fireworks and matches.

Water from volcanic areas is rich in minerals. It is bottled and sold, because people like to drink it for their health.

A geothermal power station in Iceland

Write On...

Imagine having a debate about living on a volcano. How would you build the argument if you were speaking **for** it? And what points would you make if you had to speak **against** it?

Studying volcanoes

We cannot stop volcanoes erupting – but we can limit their damage. Scientists who study volcanoes help with this. Their knowledge means they can predict when eruptions are going to happen.

Volcanic scientists are called vulcanologists. They visit active volcanoes and collect samples of gas, lava and ash. They can recognise the signs that an eruption will happen soon. By studying old lava or ash, they can work out where lava and ash from a new eruption might go.

Protective clothes

Being a volcanic scientist is dangerous. Vulcanologists wear hard hats to protect against lava bombs, special suits that reflect the heat, sturdy boots and heat-resistant gloves. They sometimes have to wear gas masks, too.

Super-tough robots can go where human vulcanologists can't – they can even be lowered into a volcano's crater to collect samples and take pictures!

A vulcanologist climbs out of the crater of Nyiragongo, an active volcano in central Africa.

Earthquakes can be a sign that an eruption is on its way. Vulcanologists measure earthquakes with instruments called seismographs.

Write On...

Writing in the first person (as **I**) can make what you describe feel more real. Finish an account by a vulcanologist that starts: **I scrambled up the slope towards the glowing red lava...**

Write On... Writing school

Are you ready to show off some of the terrific volcano facts you've found out? First, decide on your form. Here are some ideas:

 A diary about a volcano becoming more and more active, written by a child who lives on its slopes.

 An encyclopedia article about the volcano Krakatoa. Search online or in a library book to find out about its epic eruption in 1883.

 A film script about a family that gets split up during a volcanic eruption – and how they all find each other again.

 Try telling a story through a comic strip, like the one below about the Mexican volcanoes Popocatépetl (say: *Po-po-cat-e-pet-al*) and Iztaccihuatl (say: *Is-tax-e-wot-ul*):

AN AZTEC WARRIOR CALLED POPOCATÉPETL WANTED TO MARRY A PRINCESS CALLED IZTACCIHUATL. HER DAD SAID HE MUST FIGHT A WAR FIRST.

THE PRINCESS THOUGHT THAT POPOCATÉPETL HAD DIED IN BATTLE. BY THE TIME HE RETURNED, SHE HAD DIED OF A BROKEN HEART.

THE GODS TURNED THE LOVERS INTO VOLCANOES. POPOCATÉPETL SPITS OUT ASH WHEN HE REMEMBERS HIS PRINCESS'S DEATH.

Why not write an advertising leaflet, trying to persuade holidaymakers to visit Pompeii. Be really persuasive.

Find pictures for your leaflet online or in a travel brochure.

VISIT POMPEII!

Travel back in time to the holiday of a lifetime!

Visit the ancient Roman city of Pompeii, preserved forever by the violent eruption of the volcano Vesuvius.

Explore ancient Roman streets and buildings.

See stunning mosaics and fabulous frescoes!

Encounter Roman families, captured just as they looked at the moment disaster struck.

Vesuvius looms on the horizon.

Glossary

active Describes a volcano that is erupting or has erupted in the last few centuries.

archaeologist Someone who digs things up to find out about people in the past.

bacterium (pl: bacteria) A tiny living thing made up of just one cell.

black smoker A vent on the ocean bed that is releasing hot, black water.

caldera A ring-shaped hollow formed by a volcano collapsing.

crater The wide opening at the top of a volcano's vent, where lava is thrown out.

crust The rocky surface of the Earth.

dormant Describes a volcano that has not erupted in the last few centuries but could erupt again.

extinct Describes a volcano that will never erupt again.

forge A place where metal objects are made.

fresco A picture painted on a wall or ceiling before the plaster is dry.

fumarole A jet of steam that escapes from a crack in the Earth.

geothermal energy Heat energy from inside the Earth.

geyser A jet of hot water and steam, caused by volcanic activity, that shoots out of the ground every so often.

hot spot An area of magma under the Earth's crust, away from any plate boundaries.

lava Molten rock that flows out of a volcano.

magma Molten rock inside the Earth.

mosaic A picture or design made from small coloured pieces of stone or glass.

mudflow A river of mud that flows down a volcano, also called a lahar.

mythology A collection of stories called myths that belong to one religion or culture. Myths often star gods, heroes or monsters, and may blend fact and fiction.

pillow lava Lava that cools underwater, forming pillow-shaped lumps.

plate Short for tectonic plate. One of the huge sections of rock that fit together to make up the Earth's crust.

pyroclastic flow A rushing river of rock, gas and ash released by an eruption.

tsunami A huge tidal wave, often caused by a volcanic eruption or earthquake.

VEI Volcanic Explosivity Index, a scale that measures volcanic eruptions.

vulcanologist A scientist who studies volcanoes.

Further reading and websites

READ MORE ABOUT VOLCANOES:
100 Facts: Volcanoes by Chris Oxlade (Miles Kelly Publishing, 2012)

Catastrophe: Volcano Disasters by John Hawkins (Franklin Watts, 2014)

Where on Earth? Volcanoes and Earthquakes by Susie Brooks (Wayland, 2015)

READ MORE ABOUT BEING A GREAT WRITER:
How to Write a Story by Simon Cheshire (Bloomsbury, 2014)

How to Write Your Best Story Ever! by Christopher Edge (Oxford University Press, 2015)

The Usborne Write Your Own Story Book (Usborne Publishing, 2011)

DISCOVER MORE ABOUT VOLCANOES ONLINE:
www.bbc.co.uk/science/earth/natural_disasters/volcano
Stunning TV clips of volcanic eruptions.

www.ngkids.co.uk/science-and-nature/Volcano-Facts
Awesome volcano facts and videos from National Geographic Kids.

www.onegeology.org/extra/kids/volcanoes
Information about volcanoes from a specialist earth science organisation.

Index

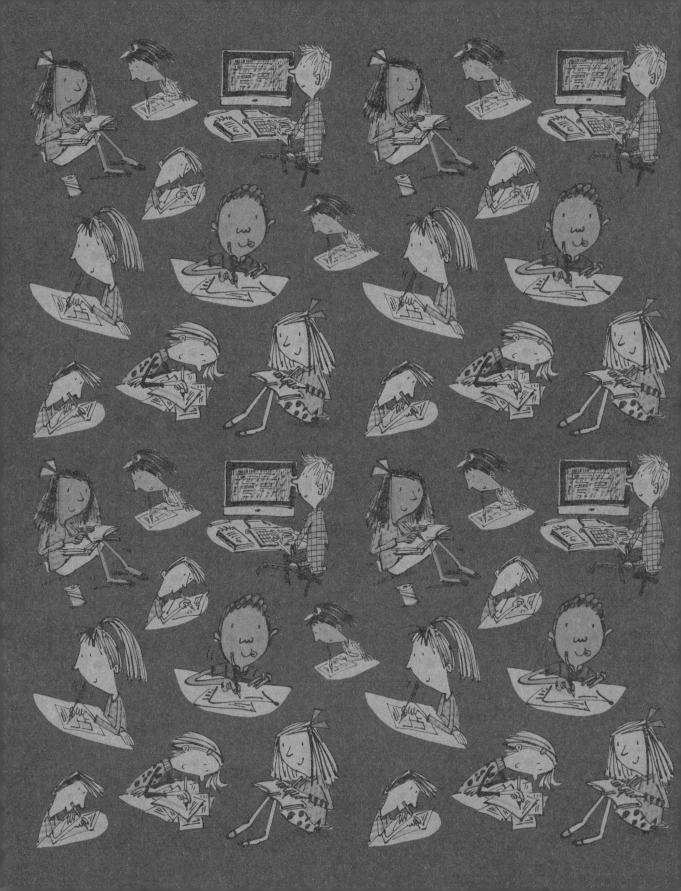